Merry Christmas,
Tyler.

Last book of the
20th. Century!

Love,
Grama Dixie

-99-

THE MAKE-SOMETHING CLUB IS BACK!

Skipper   Tag   Winky

THE MAKE-SOMETHING CLUB IS BACK!

MORE FUN WITH CRAFTS, FOOD, AND GIFTS

By Frances Zweifel

Illustrated by Ann Schweninger

Viking

To Hannah and Benjamin, the Next Generation
—F. Z.

For Deborah Brodie
—A. S.

VIKING
Published by the Penguin Group
Penguin Books USA Inc., 375 Hudson Street, New York, New York 10014, U.S.A.
Penguin Books Ltd, 27 Wrights Lane, London W8 5TZ, England
Penguin Books Australia Ltd, Ringwood, Victoria, Australia
Penguin Books Canada Ltd, 10 Alcorn Avenue, Toronto, Ontario, Canada M4V 3B2
Penguin Books (N.Z.) Ltd, 182–190 Wairau Road, Auckland 10, New Zealand

Penguin Books Ltd, Registered Offices: Harmondsworth, Middlesex, England

First published in 1996 by Viking, a division of Penguin Books USA Inc.

1 3 5 7 9 10 8 6 4 2

LIBRARY OF CONGRESS CATALOGING-IN-PUBLICATION DATA
Zweifel, Frances W.
The Make-Something Club is back! : more fun with crafts, foods, and gifts /
by Frances Zweifel ; illustrated by Ann Schweninger.   p.   cm.
Summary : A how-to guide for projects younger children can make such
as an ant farm in a jar and pomanders from fruit.
ISBN 0-670-86727-6
1. Handicraft—Juvenile literature.   2. Cookery—Juvenile literature.
[1. Handicraft. 2. Cookery.]   I. Schweninger, Ann, ill.   II. Title.
TT160.Z395 1997 745.5—dc20   96-21438 CIP AC

Manufactured in China
Set in Egyptian 505

CONTENTS

Meet Winky, Skipper, and Tag 6–7

JANUARY . . . . Something for a Dark Day 8–9

FEBRUARY . . . . . . Something for a Snack 10–11

MARCH . . . . Something Growing 12–13

APRIL . . . . Something to Play With 14–15

MAY . . . . Something for Lunch 16–17

JUNE . . . . Something Alive 18–19

JULY . . . . Something Fun to Do 20–21

AUGUST . . . . Something Musical 22–23

SEPTEMBER . . . . . Something Sweet 24–25

OCTOBER . . . . Something Pretty 26–27

NOVEMBER . . . . . Something to Play In 28–29

DECEMBER . . . . . . Something to Give 30–31

Tips for More Fun 32

**Meet Winky,
Skipper, and Tag**

JANUARY

Something for a Dark Day

Light-Catcher Punch Pictures

Materials: roll of aluminum foil, felt tip marker, sharp pencil, towel

Directions:

1. Tear off a piece of foil about 24 inches long.

2. Fold it into thirds, with the shiny side out.

3. To make your picture stronger, fold one edge of the foil in about half an inch, and pinch it together. Do the same to the opposite edge.

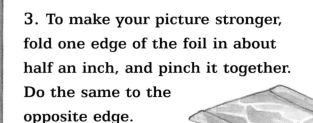

4. Lay the foil flat. With the marker, draw a simple outline design, such as a star, on the foil.

5. Fold the towel and put it on the table or floor. Place the foil flat on the towel. Carefully poke the point of the pencil through the foil, following the drawn lines. Make the holes about 1/2 inch apart and about the size of a small pea.

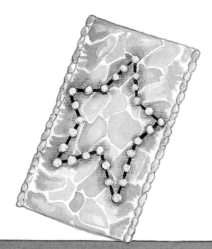

6. Hold the light-catcher to the window or a lamp to see the design. In a dark room, shine a flashlight against your light-catcher and tilt the foil to make the light picture move around the room.

Light-Catcher
Punch Pictures

Something for a Snack

Honey-Butter Toasties

Ingredients: 1 slice of bread for each snacker, 1/4 cup butter or margarine at room temperature, 3 tablespoons honey or pancake syrup (this makes enough for 6 slices)

Materials: small bowl or cup, measuring cup, tablespoon, small spoon for mixing, toaster, table knife, plate

Directions:

1. Mix the honey (or syrup) and butter (or margarine) in a small bowl.

2. Stir with the small spoon until creamy and smooth.

3. Toast the bread slices.

4. While the toast is still warm, spread some honey-butter mixture on each slice.

5. Cut each slice from corner to corner into 4 triangles.

6. Put the Honey-Butter Toasties on the plate and pass them around.

This is our best snack ever!

You always say that.

Is there any more?

Honey-Butter Toasties

MARCH
Something Growing

Spring is almost here.

And new plants will grow.

Let's grow new plants now, in the kitchen.

Kitchen Plants

Materials: carrot top with 1/2 inch of carrot left on, small sweet potato, a few dried beans, toothpicks, paper towel, jar for sweet potato, saucer for carrot, small jar with lid for beans

Directions:

1. Put the carrot top in a saucer with just enough water to cover the bottom and keep the carrot wet. Set in a sunny window.

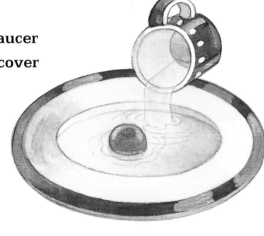

2. Push 4 toothpicks into the sweet potato around the middle. Suspend the sweet potato on the rim of a water-filled jar, so the bottom inch of the potato is in water. Set in a sunny window.

3. Take a wet (not dripping) paper towel; push it loosely into a small jar so that it fills the jar. Add a little water in the bottom to keep the paper damp. Push two beans into the jar between the wet paper and the glass. Put the top on the jar. Set in a sunny window.

4. Make sure the paper towel stays damp. Make sure water covers the bottoms of the sweet potato and the carrot. Watch for a week to see the plants sprout and grow.

Look, Winky, our carrot is growing!

And the sweet potato has roots!

Kitchen Plants

Puzzles

Materials: breakfast cereal boxes with pictures on the front, pencil, scissors

Directions:

1. Cut out the front of a cereal box.

2. On the back of the cutout box front, draw wavy lines from side to side and from top to bottom. Space them evenly so you make little squares. Make big spaces for an easy puzzle, small spaces for a harder puzzle.

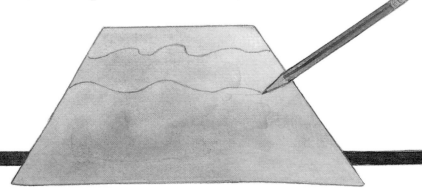

3. Cut along the pencil lines.

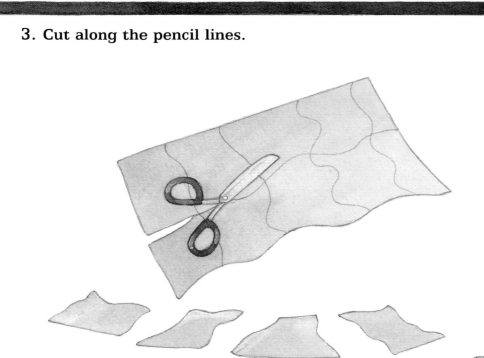

4. Turn the pieces over and match them up to make the picture again.

Puzzles

Something for Lunch

Roll-up Sandwiches

Ingredients: slices of fresh bread, various sandwich fillings—such as cheese slices, sweet pickles cut in strips, sliced olives, cream-cheese spread, jelly, butter

Materials: plate, rolling pin, table knife for spreading, toothpicks

Directions:

1. Put a slice of bread on the table and roll it out thin and flat with the rolling pin.

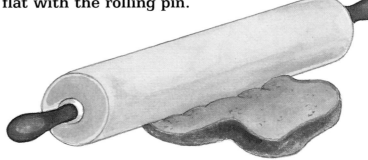

2. Spread the flattened bread with whatever filling you like.

3. Carefully roll up the bread from one edge. Stick in a toothpick to hold the roll together.

4. Put the roll-up sandwiches on a plate. Put the plate and cartons or cups of milk or juice on a tray or in a basket, and take it all outside to eat. (Do not eat the toothpicks!)

Roll-up Sandwiches

Something Alive

Ant Town

Materials: a medium- to large-size jar with a lid, a jelly glass or small jar without a lid, a small jar with a lid, sandy soil, spoon, ants, 1/2 teaspoon sugar-water, some birdseed or grass seeds

Directions:

1. Place the small jar with no lid upside down inside the large jar.

2. Carefully pour sandy soil into the jar, all around and slightly over the top of the upside-down jar inside, until it is covered.

3. Find ants by looking under flat stones or along a path. If you see ants carrying their white eggs, gently scoop some up with the spoon and drop them into the small jar with lid. Take the ants from one place only—ants from two places will kill each other. Carefully pour the ants into the large jar.

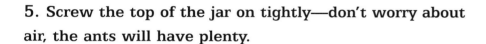

4. Drop 1 or 2 drops of sugar-water and a few seeds into the jar.

5. Screw the top of the jar on tightly—don't worry about air, the ants will have plenty.

6. Keep the jar away from direct sunlight. Watch the Ant Town for a week to see if the ants build tunnels in the soil. Then put the ants back where you found them.

Ant Town

Something Fun to Do

Soap Bubbles

Materials: baking pan filled with 1/2 inch water, about 1/4 cup of liquid soap or detergent (to make larger bubbles use more soap in the water), spoon to stir with, various blowers—such as a funnel, paper cup with a hole punched in the bottom, wire loop on a handle, piece of tubing, a straw

Directions:

1. Pour the soap into the water and mix gently. To make the bubbles last longer, chill the mixture a while.

2. Dip the wire loop, the larger end of the funnel or paper cup, or either end of the tube or straw into the soap mixture. Wave the wire loop in the air; blow gently into the end of the funnel, cup, tube, or straw you didn't dip.

Soap Bubbles

Something Musical

Kazoo Band

Materials: cardboard tubes from empty toilet-paper and paper-towel rolls, waxed paper, scissors, rubber bands, paints or felt-tip markers if desired

Directions:
1. If you want fancy kazoos, decorate the tubes first with markers or paints. Let the paint dry.

2. Tear off a sheet of waxed paper about 12 inches long. Cut it into 4 squares.

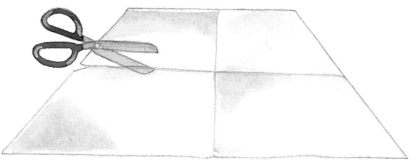

3. Fold a square of waxed paper around one end of a tube, and hold it tightly in place with a rubber band.

4. Hum a tune into the open end of the tube, saying "zooo, zooo, zooo" as you hum so the tube makes a buzzing noise.

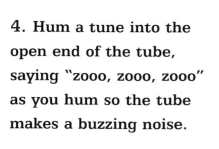

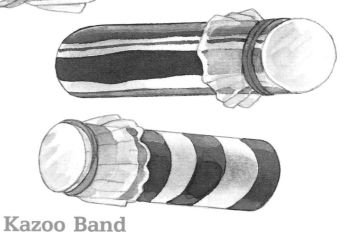

Kazoo Band

SEPTEMBER

Something Sweet

Crunchy Stuffed Dates

Ingredients: 12 or more pitted dates, 1/2 cup smooth peanut butter, 2 tablespoons crumbled crisp Chinese noodles (or chopped nuts or crisp rice cereal)

Materials: cup, spoon, measuring cup, tablespoon, plate, scissors, table knife

Directions:

1. With the scissors, cut each date open along one side. Put the dates on the plate.

2. Mix the peanut butter and crumbled noodles in the cup.

3. Open a date and spread a little peanut-butter mixture inside; press the date closed. Repeat with all the dates.

4. Pass the plate around to your friends.

Crunchy Stuffed Dates

Something Pretty

Rainbow Jars

Materials: small jars with lids, water, food coloring

Directions:

1. Working outside, on layers of newspaper spread on a work table, or at the kitchen sink, fill the jars with plain water.

2. Put a few drops of a different color into each jar. You can put 2 colors in a jar to mix a new color, such as 2 drops of yellow and 3 drops of red to make orange. Try other mixtures.

3. Put lids tightly on the jars. Dry the outside of the jars and place them on a sunny windowsill so the sun shines through them.

Rainbow Jars

Something to Play In

Play Cave / House

Materials: blanket or sheet, snap clothespins or large safety pins, a small table or 4 chairs

Directions:
1. Drape the blanket over the table. Pull up one edge for a door, and hold it open with clothespins or safety pins.

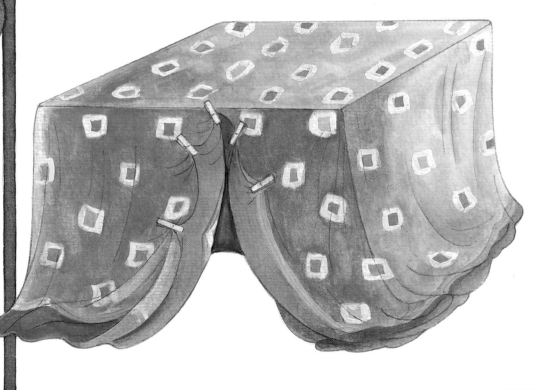

2. For a chair cave, arrange the chairs in a square with the backs facing in.

3. Drape the blanket over the chairs and hold it in place with clothespins or safety pins.

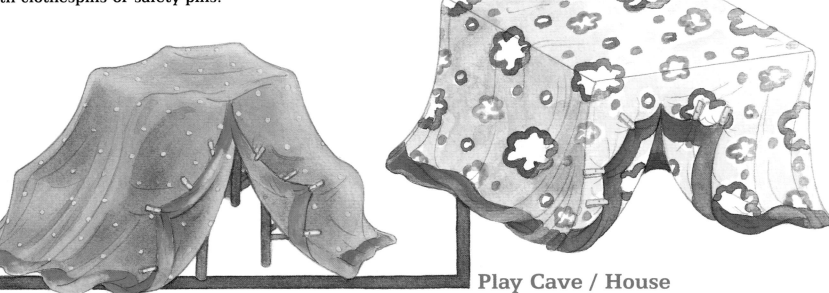

Play Cave / House

DECEMBER

Something to Give

Let's make something really good, to give away.

To look good? Or taste good? Or smell good?

Pomanders smell wonderful!

What is this nail for?

To poke holes in the orange, so we can stick the cloves in.

Pomanders

Materials: oranges or lemons, box of whole cloves, thin nail, small paper bag, 1 teaspoon each of powdered cinnamon and nutmeg, wide shallow bowl, 2 feet of narrow ribbon or a square of netting material, as from an onion bag, for each ball.

Directions:

1. With the nail, poke holes in a piece of fruit, all over it or in a pattern.

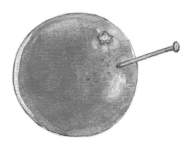

2. Gently poke a whole clove, stem first, into each hole.

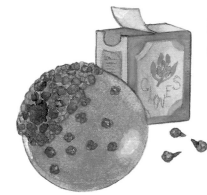

3. Mix powdered cinnamon and nutmeg in the paper bag.

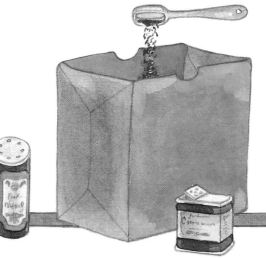

4. Carefully place one piece of fruit in the bag and shake very gently.

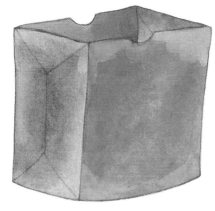

5. Place the fruit in a shallow bowl. Repeat with each fruit. Allow the fruit to dry for 2 or 3 weeks.

After they dry, you can leave the pomanders in the bowl to perfume your house, or tie them in squares of netting or tie ribbons around them for hanging in a closet.

Pomanders

TIPS FOR MORE FUN

Safety Tips: For small children, knives should be dull and scissors should have blunt tips. An adult should do all slicing and chopping of ingredients. Ant-gathering should have adult supervision, as should the use of the toaster and all glass containers.

Materials: Recipe ingredients can be substituted; for example, you can use applesauce in place of jelly, or slices of apple instead of dates. You can improvise with household items, too, if those called for are not available. For instance, use cracker or cookie boxes or any other thin cardboard with pictures to cut up for puzzles.

Adult Help: Small children may need help in measuring ingredients, poking nails into oranges, tying ribbons, and washing up. An adult may also have to help decide whose turn it is next and where to put the finished crafts.